A complete spelling programme
Year 6

raintree
Babcock ldp

Raintree is an imprint of Capstone Global Library Limited, a company incorporated in England and Wales having its registered office at 7 Pilgrim Street, London, EC4V 6LB –
Registered company number: 6695582

www.raintree.co.uk
myorders@raintree.co.uk

Text © Capstone Global Library Limited 2016
The moral rights of the proprietor have been asserted.

All rights reserved. No part of this publication may be reproduced in any form or by any means (including photocopying or storing it in any medium by electronic means and whether or not transiently or incidentally to some other use of this publication) without the written permission of the copyright owner, except in accordance with the provisions of the Copyright, Designs and Patents Act 1988 or under the terms of a licence issued by the Copyright Licensing Agency, Saffron House, 6–10 Kirby Street, London EC1N 8TS (www.cla.co.uk). Applications for the copyright owner's written permission should be addressed to the publisher.

Edited by Clare Lewis
Designed by Richard Parker and HL Studios
Picture research by Eric Gohl
Production by Helen McCreath
Originated by Capstone Global Library Ltd
Printed in China

ISBN 978 1 4747 1002 2
19 18 17 16
10 9 8 7 6 5 4

Pack
ISBN 978 1 4747 0981 1
19 18 17 16
10 9 8 7 6 5 4

British Library Cataloguing in Publication Data
A full catalogue record for this book is available from the British Library.

Acknowledgements
National Curriculum extract p. 11 © Crown copyright information licensed under the Open Government Licence v3.0.

All images provided by Shutterstock

Every effort has been made to contact copyright holders of material reproduced in this book. Any omissions will be rectified in subsequent printings if notice is given to the publisher.

All the Internet addresses (URLs) given in this book were valid at the time of going to press. However, due to the dynamic nature of the Internet, some addresses may have changed, or sites may have changed or ceased to exist since publication. While the author and publisher regret any inconvenience this may cause readers, no responsibility for any such changes can be accepted by either the author or the publisher.

Contents

Introduction	4
What is the *No Nonsense Spelling* Programme?	4
Assessment	6
Complementary resources	7
Learning spellings	9
Year 6 National Curriculum requirements	12
Year 6 Lesson plans	13
Year 6 Term 1 overview	13
Block 1 – autumn first half term	15
Block 2 – autumn second half term	20
Year 6 Term 2 overview	25
Block 3 – spring first half term	27
Block 4 – spring second half term	32
Year 6 Term 3 overview	36
Block 5 – summer first half term	38
Block 6 – summer second half term	43
Statutory word list for Years 5 and 6	48
Year 6 Supporting Resources	49

Introduction

What is the *No Nonsense Spelling* Programme?

The *No Nonsense Spelling* Programme was devised to offer teachers a comprehensive yet accessible progression in the teaching of spelling. Guidance, rather than prescription, is provided on how to teach the strategies, knowledge and skills pupils need to learn.

The focus of the programme is on the *teaching* of spelling, which embraces knowledge of spelling conventions – patterns and rules; but integral to the teaching is the opportunity to promote the *learning* of spellings, including statutory words, common exceptions and personal spellings.

The programme

- delivers a manageable tool for meeting the requirements of the 2014 National Curriculum
- has a clear progression through blocks of teaching units across the year
- comprehensively explains how to teach spelling effectively.

How *No Nonsense Spelling* is organised

The programme consists of the following elements:

- The requirements of the National Curriculum, which have been organised into strands and then broken down into termly overviews. The overall pathway can be found on the USB stick.
- Termly overviews that have been mapped across weeks as half termly plans. These follow a model of five spelling sessions across two weeks, except in Year 2 where sessions are daily.
- Daily lesson plans for each session, with Supporting Resources, including word lists and guidance on conventions.

The lesson plans

The lessons themselves then follow the structure below:

Lesson	Reference to year group, block of lessons and lesson number in sequence
Lesson type	Revise/Teach/Learn/Practise/Apply/Assess
Lesson focus	The particular spelling focus for the day
Resources needed	A list of the resources that will be needed. These might be documents that are photocopied or printed in advance so that flashcards can be prepared, or presentations to display the task/activity on a whiteboard. The resources are featured at the end of each book for reference. Editable versions are available on the USB stick, which can be copied and pasted into your own documents and edited.
Teaching activity	Key teaching points, sometimes including extra notes and tips for the teacher

Each lesson is approximately 10 to15 minutes long, but lesson plans are flexible so that the teaching can reflect the extra time needed on a teaching point if required. The Supporting Resources at the back of each book can be used as appropriate to adjust the pace and focus of the lesson. Each lesson clearly signposts when additional resources from the Programme can be used.

Supporting Resources

The Supporting Resources include pictures and word lists, which can be photocopied and made into flashcards or used in classroom displays, and pictures. They also include games and quizzes. The Resources are featured at the end of each book for reference and as editable Word documents on the USB stick, which can be copied and pasted to be used on classroom whiteboards and in other documents.

Teaching sequence

The programme has been written broadly following a teaching sequence for spelling, whereby each new concept is taught, practised and then applied and assessed. Frequently there is also a 'Revise' session before the teaching session. A typical teaching sequence is as follows:

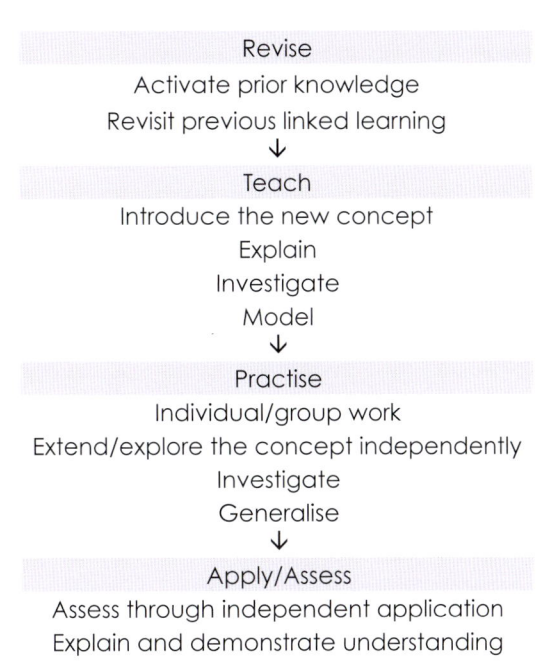

Revise
Activate prior knowledge
Revisit previous linked learning
↓
Teach
Introduce the new concept
Explain
Investigate
Model
↓
Practise
Individual/group work
Extend/explore the concept independently
Investigate
Generalise
↓
Apply/Assess
Assess through independent application
Explain and demonstrate understanding

Within the lessons, the particular focus is identified, followed by suggested teaching strategies.

By integrating activities for handwriting, the benefit of making a spelling activity kinaesthetic is secured. The pupil acquires the physical memory of the spelling pattern as well as the visual. Integral to the process is the scope to encourage pupils to learn spellings. The value of a school policy and possible approaches are explored further on page 9, 'Learning spellings'.

You will find the following referred to in the lessons:
Modelling: An activity is described, and it is anticipated that the action expected of pupils is modelled to them first.
Spelling partners: Pupils are asked to work in pairs, often to 'test' each other. They will be asked to work with their spelling partner from time to time.

Assessment

Pupils' learning is assessed throughout the programme. The 'Apply' part of the sequence regularly includes assessment activities to identify if pupils have learnt the key concept taught. These activities include:

- Testing – by teacher and peers
- Dictation
- Explaining
- Independent application in writing
- Frequent learning and testing of statutory and personal words.

Error Analysis

Error Analysis can be used to assess what strategies pupils are using in their day-to-day writing. It can also help identify where to put emphasis in the programme – for the whole class, groups or individuals. Error Analysis can also be repeated to assess progress over a longer period of time.

A template for a suggested grid for Error Analysis can be found in the Supporting Resources.

How to complete an Error Analysis:

1 Choose one piece of independent writing from each pupil.
2 Identify all the spelling errors and record them on the grid. Decide what you think is the main source of the error and record the word in the corresponding column. It is a good idea to record the word as the pupil has spelt it.
3 Identify any patterns. Quite quickly you will be able to see which aspect of spelling needs to be addressed.

The headings on the grid included are

- Common exception words
- GPCs (grapheme–phoneme correspondences) including rarer GPCs and vowel digraphs
- Homophones
- Prefixes and suffixes
- Word endings
- Other.

These headings correspond to key strands within the National Curriculum. These could be changed or further areas added if needed.

Year					
Common exception words	GPC (includes rare GPCs and vowel digraphs)	Homophones	Prefixes and suffixes	Word endings	Others
firend whent	perants for Clouser (closer) flow (flew) amzing nealy eaven	their (there) x2.	phond horrerfied		orgooment argement

Complementary resources

To support the teaching, additional resources are recommended and referred to throughout the programme.

Spelling journals	Developing the use of spelling journals can support both teachers and pupils in many ways. They enable • pupils to take responsibility for their spelling learning • pupils to refer back to previous learning • teachers to see how pupils are tackling tricky bits of spelling • teachers and pupils to discuss spelling with parents and carers Spelling journals can take many forms and are much more than just a word book. Spelling journals can be used for • practising strategies • learning words • recording rules/conventions/generalisations as an aide-memoire • word lists of really tricky words (spelling enemies) • 'Having a go' at the point of writing • ongoing record of statutory words learnt • investigations • recording spelling targets or goals • spelling tests. In the programme, there is flexibility for journals to be set up in a variety of ways. Below are a few recommendations: • Make sure that the journal can be used flexibly. A blank exercise book gives much more scope for pupils to try out ideas and organise their learning than a heavily structured format. • Model different ways of using the journal. A class spelling journal or examples from different pupils could be used to do this. • Give time for pupils to use their journals and to review them. • Do the majority of spelling work in the journal.

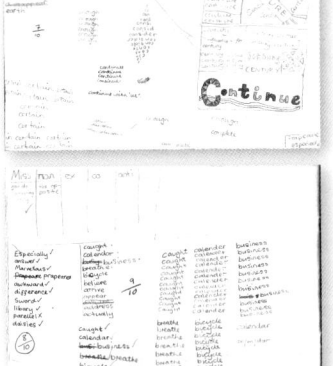

Have a go sheets	These are a key component of Strategies at the point of writing. They are introduced in the Year 2 programme and then revisited in Years 3, 4, 5 and 6. Schools need to decide how Have a go will form part of their spelling policy, together with the use of spelling journals and establishing routines for attempting unknown spellings. A Have a go sheet template is provided in the Supporting Resources. Have a go sheets can take several different forms, for example: • a large sheet of paper on a table that pupils write on when they need to. • sheets stuck in all pupils' books that fold out when pupils are writing • a book placed on the table open at a clean sheet for pupils to use. • a page in pupils' spelling journals. **Note:** it is important that teachers have an enlarged version of a Have a go sheet displayed for modelling when writing in any curriculum area and at any time in the school day. Introducing Have a Go: 1. Model writing a sentence and being unsure about how to spell a word. Talk about the tricky part in the word and some of the choices you might have for that part. You could refer to a GPC chart to find the choices if appropriate. 2. Model writing the word with two or three choices on your own enlarged version of a Have a go sheet and then model choosing the one that you think looks right and using it in your sentence. It is important that pupils learn to ask themselves the question 'Does it look right?' or 'Have I seen it like this in a book?' to help them make their choices. 3. If you are still unsure of the spelling, put a wiggly line under it in the sentence to signal that this needs checking by the teacher, or the pupil if appropriate, during proofreading time. 4. Model continuing with writing and *not* checking the correct version of the spelling at this point. This is important so that the flow of writing is not unnecessarily slowed. 5. Make sure you model this process briefly in writing in all curriculum areas. 6. Pupils use their own Have a Go sheet (or group sheet) whenever they write and refer to GPC charts and other classroom displays as support, as well as specific strategies that have been taught for using at the point of writing. 7. Remind them never to make more than three attempts at a word. Misspelt words will need to be corrected in line with your school's spelling and marking policy. Some of these words may be included in pupils' individual word lists for learning. To see lessons where Have a go strategies are first introduced, please refer to Year 2 Block 1 Lessons 11 and 17.
GPC (grapheme-phoneme correspondence) choices chart	The teaching of spelling complements very much the teaching of phonics. It is anticipated that the school will draw upon the GPC charts used in their phonics programme to work alongside the teaching of spelling.

Individual whiteboards	Individual whiteboards these can be used in a variety of ways to support lessons including checking spelling attempts, Quickwrite and Have a go.
Working wall	It is really useful to have a small area of display space in the classroom that can reflect current teaching focuses and provide support for pupils' spelling as they write. GPC charts, reminders of common spelling patterns or conventions and tricky words to remember could be part of a working wall for spelling.

Learning spellings

A school policy can help inform

- the strategies for learning spellings that are being taught
- routines for learning spellings
- links with home learning.

Learning needs to happen in school and at home. There is little evidence, though, that the traditional practice of learning spellings (usually 10) at home and being tested on them (usually on a Friday) is effective. However, there is a high expectation within the new National Curriculum that pupils will learn many increasingly complex words. Within the programme, learning spellings is built into each six-week block. Within the sessions a range of strategies for learning spellings are introduced and practised. This enables pupils to choose the strategies they find most effective for learning different words.

Tips for learning spellings at home

Learning at home needs to be an extension of the practice in school. Consider

- limiting the number of words to five or less a week to ensure success and enable deeper learning
- making sure pupils and parents have access to the range of learning strategies which have been taught in school, to use in home learning
- assessing spellings in context, for example: learning spellings in a given sentence, generating sentences for each word, assessing through unseen dictated sentences
- keeping an ongoing record of words learnt and setting very high expectations of correct application in writing once a word has been learned.

The learning strategies on the next two pages are introduced incrementally throughout the programme and can then be used to support learning spellings at home.

Look, say, cover, write, check	This is probably the most common strategy used to learn spellings. **Look**: first look at the whole word carefully and if there is one part of the word that is difficult, look at that part in more detail. **Say**: say the word as you look at it, using different ways of pronouncing it if that will make it more memorable. **Cover**: cover the word. **Write**: write the word from memory, saying the word as you do so. **Check**: Have you got it right? If yes, try writing it again and again! If not, start again – look, say, cover, write, check.
Trace, copy and replicate (and then check)	This is a similar learning process to 'look, say, cover, write, check' but is about developing automaticity and muscle memory. Write the word out on a sheet of paper ensuring that it is spelt correctly and it is large enough to trace over. Trace over the word and say it at the same time. Move next to the word you have just written and write it out as you say it. Turn the page over and write the word as you say it, and then check that you have spelt it correctly. If this is easy, do the same process for two different words at the same time. Once you have written all your words this way and feel confident, miss out the tracing and copying or the tracing alone and just write the words.
Segmentation strategy	The splitting of a word into its constituent phonemes in the correct order to support spelling.
Quickwrite	Writing the words linked to the teaching focus with speed and fluency. The aim is to write as many words as possible within a time constraint. Pupils can write words provided by the teacher or generate their own examples. For example, in two minutes write as many words as possible with the /iː/ phoneme. This can be turned into a variety of competitive games including working in teams and developing relay race approaches.
Drawing around the word to show the shape	Draw around the words making a clear distinction in size where there are ascenders and descenders. Look carefully at the shape of the word and the letters in each box. Now try to write the word making sure that you get the same shape. t o t a l l y

Drawing an image around the word	This strategy is all about making a word memorable. It links to meaning in order to try to make the spelling noticeable.

Monarchy (illustrated with stick figures and crowns)

You can't use this method as your main method of learning spellings, but it might work on those that are just a little more difficult to remember. |
| **Words without vowels** | This strategy is useful where the vowel choices are the challenge in the words. Write the words without the vowels and pupils have to choose the correct grapheme to put in the space. For example, for the word *field*:

f_____ld |
| **Pyramid words** | This method of learning words forces you to think of each letter separately.

p
py
pyr
pyra
pyram
pyrami
pyramid

You can then reverse the process so that you end up with a diamond. |
| **Other strategies** | Other methods can include:

- Rainbow writing. Using coloured pencils in different ways can help to make parts of words memorable. You could highlight the tricky part s of the word or write the tricky part in a different colour. You could also write each letter in a different colour, or write the word in red, then overlay in orange, yellow and so on.
- Making up memorable 'silly sentences' containing the word
- Saying the word in a funny way – for example, pronouncing the 'silent' letters in a word
- Clapping and counting to identify the syllables in a word. |

Year 6 National Curriculum requirements

Pupils should be taught to
- develop a range of personal strategies for learning new and irregular words*
- develop a range of personal strategies for spelling at the point of composition*
- develop a range of strategies for checking and proofreading spellings after writing*
- use further prefixes and suffixes and understand the guidance for adding them
- spell some words with 'silent' letters (rarer GPCs, for example: *knight, psalm, solemn*)
- continue to distinguish between homophones and other words which are often confused
- use knowledge of morphology and etymology in spelling and understand that the spelling of some words needs to be learnt specifically, as listed in English Appendix 1
- use dictionaries to check the spelling and meaning of words
- use the first three or four letters of a word to check spelling, meaning or both of these in a dictionary
- use a thesaurus
- proofread for spelling errors.

* non-statutory

Year 6 lesson plans

Year 6 Term 1 overview

Block 1 – autumn first half term

Week 1	Lesson 1 Revise/Learn **Words from statutory word lists**	Lesson 2 Revise/Learn **Words from statutory word lists**	Lesson 3 Revise **Strategies at the point of writing: Have a go**
Week 2	Lesson 4 Practise **Strategies at the point of writing: Have a go**	Lesson 5 Revise **Words ending '-able'/ '-ably', and '-ible'/'-ibly'**	
Week 3	Lesson 6 Practise **Strategies for learning words: words ending '-able' and '-ible'**	Lesson 7 Assess **Words ending '-able' and '-ible'**	Lesson 8 Teach **Adding suffixes beginning with vowels to words ending in '-fer'**
Week 4	Lesson 9 Practise **Adding suffixes beginning with vowels to words ending in '-fer'**	Lesson 10 Assess **Adding suffixes beginning with vowels to words ending in '-fer'**	
Week 5	Lesson 11 Practise **SATS practice**	Lesson 12 Practise **SATS practice**	Lesson 13 Practise **SATS practice**
Week 6	Lesson 14 Teach **Proofreading in smaller chunks (sentences, paragraphs)**	Lesson 15 Practise **Proofreading in smaller chunks (sentences, paragraphs)**	

Block 2 – autumn second half term

Week 1	Lesson 1 Revise/Assess **Words from statutory word lists**	Lesson 2 Revise/Assess **Words from statutory word lists**	Lesson 3 Learn **Strategies for learning words: words from statutory word list**
Week 2	Lesson 4 Learn **Homophones ('ce'/'se')**	Lesson 5 Practise **Homophones ('ce'/'se')**	
Week 3	Lesson 6 Assess **Homophones ('ce'/'se'): dictation**	Lesson 7 Learn **Strategies for learning words: words from personal spelling lists**	Lesson 8 Assess **Words from personal spelling lists**
Week 4	Lesson 9 Teach **Endings that sound like /ʃəs/ spelt '-cious' or '-tious'**	Lesson 10 Practise **Endings that sound like /ʃəs/ spelt '-cious' or '-tious'**	
Week 5	Lesson 11 Assess **Endings that sound like /ʃəs/ spelt '-cious' or '-tious': dictation**	Lesson 12 Learn **Strategies for learning words: words from statutory word list**	Lesson 13 Learn **Strategies for learning words: words from statutory word list**
Week 6	Lesson 14 Assess/Learn Learn **Words from statutory word lists**	Lesson 15 Revise **Spelling learning from this term**	

Block 1 – autumn first half term

Lesson	Year 6, block 1, lesson 1
Lesson type	Revise/Learn
Lesson focus	**Words from statutory word list**
Resources needed	Statutory word lists for years 3 and 4 and Years 5 and 6 (page 48), personal spelling lists, spelling journals
Teaching activity	The purpose of this session and the following one is to begin to establish which of the statutory words pupils can spell independently. By the end of the first term, pupils need to have revised the Year 3-4 list and identified and begun to learn words from the Year 5-6 list which are not secure. Test pupils on the Year 3-4 word list over the two sessions. This could be a class test or the children could test each other in pairs. Pupils need to record any of these words that they have spelt incorrectly in their spelling journals. These words will need to be revisited regularly over the term.

Lesson	Year 6, block 1, lesson 2
Lesson type	Revise/Learn
Lesson focus	**Words from statutory word list**
Resources needed	Statutory word lists for years 3 and 4 and Years 5 and 6 (page 48), personal spelling lists, spelling journals
Teaching activity	Continue testing pupils on the Year 3-4 word list. This could be a class test or pupils could test each other in pairs. Pupils need to record any of these words which they have spelt incorrectly in their spelling journals. These words will need to be revised regularly over the term.

Lesson	Year 6, block 1, lesson 3
Lesson type	Revise
Lesson focus	**Strategies at the point of writing: Have a go**
Resources needed	Supporting Resources 6.2 (Have a go sheet) and 6.3 (GPC chart)
Teaching activity	Remind pupils how to use Have a go sheets. See Introduction, page 8, for reminders on how to use this strategy. Model writing using a Have a go sheet and remind pupils of the strategies you might use to spell the word you want. Remind them that they don't need to make more than three attempts at spelling before choosing the one they think looks right and continuing with their writing. Check that pupils know how to use a GPC chart and that they have access to one if they need it. If they are not sure they have the correct spelling, they should draw a line under the word in their writing to alert you to this fact or for them to check themselves during proofreading. Words not spelt correctly can form part of the personal list of words to learn.

Block 1 – autumn first half term

Lesson	Year 6, block 1, lesson 4
Lesson type	Practise
Lesson focus	**Strateges at the point of writing: Have a go**
Resources needed	Supporting Resource 6.2 (Have a go sheet)
Teaching activity	Using their most recent writing, pupils review their spellings and practise using the Have a go sheet. Each pupil identifies a small list of personal spellings to learn over this half term.

Lesson	Year 6, block 1, lesson 5
Lesson type	Revise
Lesson focus	**Words ending '-able'/'-ably' and '-ible'/'-ibly'**
Resources needed	Supporting Resources 6.4 (cards 'able'/'-ably' and '-ible'/'-ibly') and 6.5 (words ending '-ible' and '-able')
Teaching activity	Revisit the conventions for using '-able'/'-ably' and '-ible'/'-ibly' (see notes below). Play a game where pairs of pupils have '-able'/'-ably' and '-ible'/'-ibly' cards. The teacher reads out a word from the list provided. Pupils have to decide if the word is spelt with '-able' or '-ible'. Pupils raise the card they think is correct. Write the words on the board to check each time. Where there is disagreement, write both down and model applying the following conventions to support the decision. **Notes:** • '-able' is more common than '-ible'. • The '-able' ending is usually used (but not always) if a complete root word can be heard before it. In some cases the ending of the root word may change, for example, *rely/reliable*. • The '-ible' root is common if a complete root word cannot be heard before it (but not without exception, for example *sensible*). • The '-able' ending is used if there is a related word ending in '-ation', for example, *applicable/application*. Show how, when you add '-ibly' or '-ably', the same conventions apply as above, but you drop the 'e' from the end of the word before adding '-ibly' or '-ably'.

Block 1 – autumn first half term

Lesson	Year 6, block 1, lesson 6
Lesson type	Practise
Lesson focus	**Strategies for learning words: words ending '-able' and '-ible'**
Resources needed	Supporting Resource 6.5 (words ending '-able' and '-ible')
Teaching activity	Pupils work with a partner to learn the '-able'/'-ible' words from the last session that were tricky. They apply some of the spelling strategies they have been taught to learn the words. Pupils choose the strategy that works best for them from the following: • Pyramid words • Trace, copy and replicate • Look, say, cover, write, check • Drawing around the word to show the shape • Drawing an image around the word • Words without vowels • Any other methods that work

Lesson	Year 6, block 1, lesson 7
Lesson type	Assess
Lesson focus	**Words ending '-able' and '-ible'**
Resources needed	Spelling journals
Teaching activity	Dictate the sentences below to test the pupils' application of the conventions. Ask pupils to check with a spelling partner at the end. They record any tricky '-able'/'-ible' words in their spelling journals. *Children can be adorable, but they can also be horrible! This is reversible by the use of sensible and enjoyable lessons.* *The gingerbread house is both edible and breakable. It's also incredibly delicious.* *Handwriting needs to be legible so that words are identifiable and it is possible to read it.*

No Nonsense Spelling

No Nonsense Spelling Programme

Block 1 – autumn first half term

Lesson	Year 6, block 1, lesson 8
Lesson type	Teach
Lesson focus	**Adding suffixes beginning with vowels to words ending in '-fer'**
Resources needed	Supporting Resource 6.6 (suffix and word cards), spelling journals, individual whiteboards
Teaching activity	Revisit the common suffixes that can be added to words (see list provided). Explain to pupils that sometimes changes have to be made to the end of the root word when a suffix is added, for example changing 'y' to 'i' in *happy/happily, mercy/merciful*.

Explore what happens when we add suffixes to words ending in '–fer'. Read out the word *refer* and discuss how to spell it and what it means. If we change this word to *referral*, how would we write it? Pupils try on their whiteboards. Discuss their attempts and explain the rule.

Try with the word *prefer*, changing it to *preferring*. Now try with the word *reference*. Pupils try and then discuss why the 'r' doesn't double in this case.

Pupils note the rules in their spelling journals:

- The 'r' is doubled if the '-fer' is still stressed when the ending is added'.
- The 'r' is not doubled if the '-fer' is no longer stressed. |

Lesson	Year 6, block 1, lesson 9
Lesson type	Practise
Lesson focus	**Adding suffixes beginning with vowels to words ending in '-fer'**
Resources needed	Supporting Resource 6.6 (suffix and word cards), spelling journals
Teaching activity	Pupils work in pairs to build words by adding suffix cards to the words cards. How many real words can they make? They record in their spelling journals where the 'r' doubles and where it doesn't. At the end, share the pupil's findings as a class. Ensure that the rules have been applied correctly and that pupils understand them.

Lesson	Year 6, block 1, lesson 10
Lesson type	Assess
Lesson focus	**Adding suffixes beginning with vowels to words ending in '-fer'**
Resources needed	Spelling journals
Teaching activity	Test the spelling of the following words. *referee, referred, transferring, preference, referral, transferred*

Pupils record any words they spell incorrectly in their spelling journals. |

Block 1 – autumn first half term

Lesson	Year 6, block 1, lesson 11
Lesson type	Practise
Lesson focus	**SATs practice**
Resources needed	Exemplar materials or SATs papers (post 2016)
Teaching activity	Use exemplar materials or SATs papers (post 2016) with all pupils.

Lesson	Year 6, block 1, lessons 12 and 13
Lesson type	Practise
Lesson focus	**SATs practice**
Resources needed	Spelling journals
Teaching activity	Mark the SATs papers and then work through it with the whole class. Discuss tricky words and look at different attempts at spellings. Link words to previous teaching. Model applying different strategies to the paper, for example proofreading and Have a go. Pupils add a few of the words they spelt incorrectly to their personal lists. Identify any pupils who need further guided support with particular strategies to manage the test situation.

Lesson	Year 6, block 1, lesson 14
Lesson type	Teach
Lesson focus	**Proofreading in smaller chunks (sentences, paragraphs)**
Resources needed	Supporting resource 6.7 (checklist for spelling) spelling journals, dictionary
Teaching activity	Revisit strategies that pupils already know for proofreading their writing. Model really close proofreading by taking a paragraph from one of the pupils' writing: • Read the whole paragraph for sense. • Are there any really obvious spelling errors? • Model looking closely at each sentence in turn. Run your pen along under each word checking carefully. Put a line under any word that might be spelt incorrectly. Return to any words underlined and model using Have a go strategies, use of spelling journal notes and dictionaries to correct these spellings.

Lesson	Year 6, block 1, lesson 15
Lesson type	Practise
Lesson focus	**Proofreading in smaller chunks (sentences, paragraphs)**
Resources needed	Supporting Resource 6.7 (checklist for proofreading)
Teaching activity	All pupils choose a paragraph of their own writing and repeat the close checking modelled in the previous session. Give pupils the checklist to follow as they proofread.

Block 2 – autumn second half term

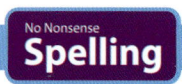

Lesson	Year 6, block 2, lessons 1 and 2
Lesson type	Revise/Assess
Lesson focus	**Words from statutory word lists**
Resources needed	Statutory word lists for Years 3 and 4 and Years 5 and 6 (page 48), spelling journals
Teaching activity	The purpose of these two sessions is to establish which of the statutory words pupils can spell independently. By the end of this term, pupils need to have revised the Year 3-4 list and identified and begun to learn words from the Year 5-6 list that are not secure. Test pupils on all of the Year 5-6 words over two sessions. This could be a class test or pupils could test each other in pairs. You will need to differentiate this testing. Pupils record any words that they have spelt incorrectly in their spelling journals. Where children are still insecure with the Year 3-4 list, they need to continue to learn these alongside a small number of the Year 5-6 words.

Lesson	Year 6, block 2, lesson 3
Lesson type	Learn
Lesson focus	**Strategies for learning words: words from statutory word lists**
Resources needed	Statutory word list (for Years 5 and 6 (page 48), personal spelling lists, spelling journals
Teaching activity	Pupils begin to learn the first set of words they have identified in the previous two sessions (no more than 6–10), using the learning strategies previously introduced: - Pyramid words - Trace, copy and replicate - Look, say, cover, write, check - Drawing around the word to show the shape - Drawing an image around the word - Words without vowels - Any other methods that work

No Nonsense Spelling

No Nonsense Spelling Programme

Block 2 – autumn second half term

Lesson	Year 6, block 2, lesson 4
Lesson type	Learn
Lesson focus	**Homophones ('ce'/'se')**
Resources needed	Supporting Resource 6.8 (sentences with homophones), spelling journals
Teaching activity	The homophones for these sessions all follow a pattern based on their word class. • Nouns are spelt with '-ce' and verbs with '-se'. • They are also sometimes pronounced slightly differently. Introduce the homophones to pupils in the context of sentences. Ask them to investigate why the words are spelt differently. Can they identify a rule to help us remember which to use? You need to make explicit links to grammar teaching in this session. Pupils record the rules in their spelling journals.

Lesson	Year 6, block 2, lesson 5
Lesson type	Practise
Lesson focus	**Homophones ('ce'/'se')**
Resources needed	Supporting Resource 6.9 (homophones list), spelling journals
Teaching activity	Pupils make up their own sentences in pairs for the homophones on the list, showing that they have understood the rule based on word class. Share their sentences at the end and use a couple to display as reminders on the working wall.

Lesson	Year 6, block 2, lesson 6
Lesson type	Assess
Lesson focus	**Homophones ('ce'/'se'): dictation**
Resources needed	Spelling journals
Teaching activity	Dictate the following sentences to check that pupils can apply the rule for spelling these words correctly: *Children have been advised that devices must be switched off in school. Ignoring this advice will result in exclusion.* *The only way to improve is to practise.* *The practice of giving red cards for dissent is common.* Discuss each sentence at the end to ensure that the correct rule has been applied and that pupils understand the word class.

Block 2 – autumn second half term

Lesson	Year 6, block 2, lesson 7
Lesson type	Learn
Lesson focus	**Strategies for learning words: words from personal spelling lists**
Resources needed	Personal spelling lists, spelling journals
Teaching activity	Pupils identify words to learn from their own writing. They record the words and learn them using the range of strategies already taught: • Pyramid words • Trace, copy and replicate • Look, say, cover, write, check • Drawing around the word to show the shape • Drawing an image around the word • Words without vowels • Any other methods that work

Lesson	Year 6, block 2, lesson 8
Lesson type	Assess
Lesson focus	**Words from personal spelling lists**
Resources needed	Spelling journals
Teaching activity	Pupils work with a partner to test spellings and identify words that still need to be learnt. You may need to provide an extra session for pupils to learn these words.

No Nonsense Spelling

No Nonsense Spelling Programme

Block 2 – autumn second half term

Lesson	Year 6, block 2, lesson 9
Lesson type	Teach
Lesson focus	**Endings that sound like /ʃəs/ spelt '-cious' or '-tious'**
Resources needed	Supporting Resource 6.10 (list of words ending '–cious' or '–tious')
Teaching activity	Introduce the sound and the two spelling patterns. Explain that these two spelling patterns sound the same so we need to investigate when to use '-tious' and when to use '-cious'. Show a few of the words and ask pupils to identify the root word. Write the root word next to the '-tious'/'-cious' word: *fiction fictitious* *vice vicious* *caution cautious* *malice malicious* What do they notice about the words that take '-cious'? Pupils record what is agreed in their spelling journals. **Notes:** • Not many common words end like this. • If the root word ends in '-ce', the ending is usually spelt with 'c', for example: *vice/vicious, grace/gracious*. • Exceptions: *anxious* and *suspicious*.

Lesson	Year 6, block 2, lesson 10
Lesson type	Practise
Lesson focus	**Endings that sound like /ʃəs/ spelt '-cious' or '-tious'**
Resources needed	Supporting Resource 6.10 (list of words ending '-cious' or '-tious')
Teaching activity	Pupils Quickwrite words with '–tious' and '-cious' endings. The teacher reads out the word and pupils write it three times in joined-up handwriting as quickly as possible. Show the correct spelling of the word and check as a class.

Lesson	Year 6, block 2, lesson 11
Lesson type	Assess
Lesson focus	**Endings that sound like /ʃəs/ spelt '-cious' or '-tious': dictation**
Resources needed	Supporting Resource 6.10 (list of words ending '-cious' or '-tious')
Teaching activity	Dictate the following sentences: *The last dragon in Middle-earth was precious yet vicious and malicious. The dwarves were suspicious and cautious of this fictitious beast. One bite was said to cause terrible, infectious boils.* Pupils check the spelling of '-cious' and '-tious' words with a spelling partner.

Block 2 – autumn second half term

Lesson	Year 6, block 2, lessons 12 and 13
Lesson type	Learn
Lesson focus	**Strategies for learning words: words from statutory word lists**
Resources needed	Statutory word list for Year 5 and 6 (page 48), spelling journals
Teaching activity	In this session and the next, pupils learn selected words from the statutory list (mainly Year 5/6 and Year 3/4 if any remain), identified at the beginning of the half term. They use the range of learning strategies previously taught. • Pyramid words • Trace, copy and replicate • Look, say, cover, write, check • Drawing around the word to show the shape • Drawing an image around the word • Words without vowels • Any other methods that work

Lesson	Year 6, block 2, lesson 14
Lesson type	Assess
Lesson focus	**Words from statutory word list**
Resources needed	Statutory word list for Years 5 and 6 (page 48), spelling journals
Teaching activity	Pupils work with partners to test each other on the statutory words that they have learnt over this half term. They update the records of spellings learnt in their spelling journals.

Lesson	Year 6, block 2, lesson 15
Lesson type	Revise
Lesson focus	**Spelling learning from this term**
Resources needed	Spelling journals, various
Teaching activity	Identify any aspects of the spelling knowledge or skills from this term's work that need to be revisited to secure. This could include further work on spelling statutory words if needed. Use key activities and resources from previous sessions to revisit these areas.

Year 6 Term 2 overview

Block 3 – spring first half term

Week 1	Lesson 1 Revise **Words with 'ough' letter string**	Lesson 2 Practise **Words with 'ough' letter string**	Lesson 3 Assess **Words with 'ough' letter string: pair testing**
Week 2	Lesson 4 Learn **Strategies for learning words: words from statutory and personal spelling lists**	Lesson 5 Learn **Strategies for learning words: words from statutory and personal spelling lists**	
Week 3	Lesson 6 Assess **Words from statutory and personal spelling lists: pair testing**	Lesson 7 Teach **Words ending '-cial' and '-tial'**	Lesson 8 Practise **Words ending '-cial' and '-tial'**
Week 4	Lesson 9 Apply **Words ending '-cial' and '-tial'**	Lesson 10 Teach **Proofreading someone else's writing**	
Week 5	Lesson 11 Learn **Strategies for learning words: words from personal spellings lists**	Lesson 12 Assess **Words from personal spellings lists: pair testing**	Lesson 13 Revise **Generating words from prefixes**
Week 6	Lesson 14 Learn **Strategies for learning words: words from statutory and personal spelling lists**	Lesson 15 Assess **All statutory words learnt so far this term**	

Block 4 – spring second half term

Week 1	Lesson 1 Revise **Spelling learning from the previous half term**	Lesson 2 Learn **Strategies for learning words: words from statutory and personal spelling lists**	Lesson 3 Learn **Strategies for learning words: words from statutory and personal spelling lists**
Week 2	Lesson 4 Assess **Words from statutory and personal spelling lists**	Lesson 5 Teach **Homophones (*dessert/desert, stationery/stationary, complement/compliment, principle/principal, prophet/profit*)**	
Week 3	Lesson 6 Revise **Homophones covered in KS2**	Lesson 7 Assess **Homophones covered in KS2: dictation**	Lesson 8 Practise **Proofreading**
Week 4	Lesson 9 Learn **Strategies for learning words: words from statutory and personal spelling lists**	Lesson 10 Assess **Words from statutory and personal spelling lists**	
Week 5	Lesson 11 Revise **Generating words from prefixes and roots**	Lesson 12 Practise/Apply **Generating words from prefixes and roots**	
Week 6	Lesson 13 Learn **Strategies for learning words: words from statutory and personal spelling lists**	Lesson 14 Assess **Words from statutory spelling lists**	

Block 3 – spring first half term

Lesson	Year 6, block 3, lesson 1
Lesson type	Revise
Lesson focus	**Words with 'ough' letter string**
Resources needed	Supporting Resource 6.11 (part of 'ough' poem)
Teaching activity	Return to a section of the pronunciation poem used in Year 5, block 1, lesson 2, Supporting Resource 5.4. Use this section as a dictation to see if pupils can apply their knowledge of the 'ough' letter string. Challenge them by explaining that there are eight words in this section containing the 'ough' letter string. Once they have written it, they can check with a spelling partner to see if they have all eight. Show the correct spelling of the poem. Ask how many different phonemes are represented by the 'ough' letter string? (There are six different phonemes.)

Lesson	Year 6, block 3, lesson 2
Lesson type	Practise
Lesson focus	**Words with 'ough' letter string**
Resources needed	Supporting Resource 6.12 (word cards with 'ough' letter string)
Teaching activity	Use sets of the 'ough' word cards. In small groups pupils play Pairs. Turn the cards over face down on the table and pupils take it in turns to turn over two cards to try to make a pair (in this case two words where 'ough' is pronounced in the same way). At the end of the session share the pairs of words that they found and see if there are any other words that could join the group of words to make more pairs.

Lesson	Year 6, block 3, lesson 3
Lesson type	Assess
Lesson focus	**Words with 'ough' letter string: pair testing**
Resources needed	Supporting Resource 6.12 (word cards with 'ough' letter string)
Teaching activity	Children work with a partner to test the 'ough' words learnt.

No Nonsense Spelling

Block 3 – spring first half term

Lesson	Year 6, block 3, lessons 4 and 5
Lesson type	Learn
Lesson focus	**Strategies for learning words: words from statutory and personal spelling lists**
Resources needed	Statutory word list for Years 5 and 6 (page 48), personal spelling lists, spelling journals
Teaching activity	The purpose of these two sessions is to establish which of the statutory words the children can spell independently. During this term, pupils need to be securing the majority of the Year 5-6 statutory word list. Pupils will have a list of words they need to learn in their spelling journals from the assessment in Term 1. Model selecting 5 to10 of these words to learn. Model applying some of the learning strategies already taught: • Pyramid words • Trace, copy and replicate • Look, say, cover, write, check • Drawing around the word to show the shape • Drawing an image around the word • Words without vowels • Any other methods that work Pupils practise learning a few of their words in the first session and continue to learn up to 10 words in the second session.

Lesson	Year 6, block 3, lesson 6
Lesson type	Assess
Lesson focus	**Selected spellings from statutory and personal word lists: pair testing**
Resources needed	Statutory word list for Years 5 and 6 (page 48), personal spelling lists for each pupil, spelling journals
Teaching activity	Pupils work in pairs and test each other on the words they have learnt in the last two sessions. They update their list of words to learn in their spelling journals.

Block 3 – spring first half term

Lesson	Year 6, block 3, lesson 7
Lesson type	Teach
Lesson focus	**Words ending '-cial' and '-tial'**
Resources needed	Supporting Resource 6.13 (table format) and 6.14 ('-cial' and '-tial' words list), dictionary
Teaching activity	Explain that we are going to explore another tricky word ending where there is a choice to make. Link back to '-tious' and '-cious' from last term (page 23). Use the table format provided to model a way of exploring the words that pupils will practise in the next session: 1 Identify the root word. 2 Explain what the word means. 3 Make a guess about why the word is spelt '-tial' or '-cial'. You will need to model using a dictionary to support both identifying the root word and finding the definition. **Notes:** - '-cial' is common after a vowel letter. - '-tial' is common after a consonant letter. - Exceptions: *initial, financial, provincial*

Lesson	Year 6, block 3, lesson 8
Lesson type	Practise
Lesson focus	**Words ending '–cial' and '–tial'**
Resources needed	Supporting Resource 6.13 (table format) and 6.14 ('-cial' and '-tial' words list), dictionary
Teaching activity	Pupils work in pairs to continue the activity modelled in the previous lesson. They should try to do as many words as possible from the list, but a minimum two '-tial' words and two '-cial' words. At the end of the session share what the pupils have discovered and try to draw any generalisations or observations about spelling choice.

Lesson	Year 6, block 3, lesson 9
Lesson type	Apply
Lesson focus	**Words ending '-cial' and '-tial'**
Resources needed	Supporting Resource 6.13 (table format) and 6.14 ('-cial' and '-tial' words list), spelling journals
Teaching activity	Pupils take the words they have investigated and write sentences including them. Ensure that the words are spelt correctly and used appropriately.

Block 3 – spring first half term

Lesson	Year 6, block 3, lesson 10
Lesson type	Teach
Lesson focus	**Proofreading someone else's writing**
Resources needed	Supporting Resource 6.15 (instructions for proofreading), pupils' writing books, spelling journals
Teaching activity	Revise strategies that pupils already know for proofreading their own writing. The focus for this session is on proofreading a partner's work. Pupils follow this process: 1 Swap writing books with your spelling partner. 2 Proofread the last two pieces of work. 3 Underline with a wiggly line any words which you think may be spelt incorrectly. 4 Feed back to your partner. 5 Work together to correct spellings. 6 Add words to learn to personal list in spelling journal. (These instructions are included on the Supporting Resource)

Lesson	Year 6, block 3, lesson 11
Lesson type	Learn
Lesson focus	**Strategies for learning words: words from personal spelling lists**
Resources needed	Personal spelling, spelling journals
Teaching activity	Pupils apply the range of learning strategies already learnt to the list of words in their spelling journal (added to in the previous proofreading session): • Pyramid words • Trace, copy and replicate • Look, say, cover, write, check • Drawing around the word to show the shape • Drawing an image around the word • Words without vowels • Any other methods that work At the end of the session, discuss ways that pupils have applied the strategies. Pupils share examples of strategies that have really helped.

Lesson	Year 6, block 3, lesson 12
Lesson type	Assess
Lesson focus	**Words from personal spelling lists: pair testing**
Resources needed	Personal spelling lists, spelling journals
Teaching activity	Pupils work with partners to test spellings and identify words which still need to be learnt. You may need to provide an extra session for pupils to learn these words.

Block 3 – spring first half term

Lesson	Year 6, block 3, lesson 13
Lesson type	Revise
Lesson focus	**Generating words from prefixes**
Resources needed	Supporting Resources 6.16 (prefix list) and 6.17 (table format), dictionary or internet, spelling journals
Teaching activity	Remind pupils about the meaning of the term 'etymology'. This lesson focuses on the etymology of prefixes and how it helps us both to spell and understand meaning. Give pairs of pupils a common prefix from the list. They need to: 1 find the meaning of the prefix and where it came from (using a dictionary or the internet) 2 find three or more words which start with that prefix and be ready to explain what those words mean based on their knowledge of the prefix. Pupils could copy the table format provided into their spelling journals. At the end of the session ask some of the pupils to explain one of the words they have found using their knowledge of the meaning of the prefix.

Lesson	Year 6, block 3, lesson 14
Lesson type	Learn
Lesson focus	**Strategies for learning words: words from statutory and personal spelling lists**
Resources needed	Statutory word list for Years 5 and 6 (page 48), personal spelling lists for each pupil, spelling journals
Teaching activity	Pupils learn spellings from their personal and statutory word lists. They use previously taught strategies to help them. You may need to direct pupils depending on how many of the statutory words they know.

Lesson	Year 6, block 3, lesson 15
Lesson type	Assess
Lesson focus	**All statutory words learnt so far this term**
Resources needed	Statutory word list for Years 5 and 6 (page 48), spelling journals
Teaching activity	Do a class test on all statutory words learnt so far this term. Identify words for further learning.

Block 4 – spring second half term

Lesson	Year 6, block 4, lesson 1
Lesson type	Revise
Lesson focus	**Spelling learning from the previous half term**
Resources needed	Statutory word list for Years 5 and 6 (page 48)
Teaching activity	Identify any aspects of the spelling knowledge or skills from this term's work that needs to be revisited to secure. This could include further work on spelling statutory words if needed. Use key activities and resources from previous sessions to revisit.

Lesson	Year 6, block 4, lessons 2 and 3
Lesson type	Learn
Lesson focus	**Strategies for learning words: words from statutory and personal spelling lists**
Resources needed	Statutory word list for Years 5 and 6 (page 48), personal spelling lists for each pupil, spelling journals
Teaching activity	All pupils should be working on words from the Year 5-6 word list by this point. Support pupils to identify a group of words they need to learn across this half term. For those pupils who found the SATs practice very difficult, ensure that the list represents words from both the Year 3-4 and Year 5-6 lists and any Year 2 common exception words that they frequently misspell. Revisit briefly the list of strategies for learning words: • Pyramid words • Trace, copy and replicate • Look, say, cover, write, check • Drawing around the word to show the shape • Drawing an image around the word • Words without vowels • Any other methods that work Pupils work independently to learn words from their lists.

Lesson	Year 6, block 4, lesson 4
Lesson type	Assess
Lesson focus	**Words from statutory and personal lists**
Resources needed	Statutory list (see page 48), personal spelling lists, spelling journals
Teaching activity	Pupils work with a partner to test spellings and identify words that still need to be learnt. You will need to support those groups who need most help in order to pass the SATs spelling element of the GPaS test.

Block 4 – spring second half term

Lesson	Year 6, block 4, lesson 5
Lesson type	Teach
Lesson focus	**Homophones (*dessert/desert, stationery/stationary, complement/compliment, principle/principal, prophet/profit*)**
Resources needed	Supporting Resource 6.18 (homophones list), spelling journals
Teaching activity	Introduce the new homophones on the list provided. In pairs, pupils discuss what the two different meanings of these words are. Pupils work with partners to think of some clever ways to remember which word is which (see the idea below). Share ideas and pupils record them in their spelling journals. **Note:** *stationery/stationary*: These words are commonly confused but there is a fun and simple trick to stop you doing the same. Whenever you mean the paper or writing supplies, think about the word *paper*, which ends in 'er'. The word you want is also spelt with 'er', not 'ar', like the word *paper*.

Lesson	Year 6, block 4, lesson 6
Lesson type	Revise
Lesson focus	**Homophones covered in KS2**
Resources needed	Supporting Resource 6.19 (homophones list for KS2)
Teaching activity	Give pupils a list of all the homophones learnt so far in KS2 to revise. They identify any that are tricky to remember and revisit or create a way of remembering them.

Lesson	Year 6, block 4, lesson 7
Lesson type	Assess
Lesson focus	**Homophones covered in KS2: dictation**
Resources needed	Supporting Resource 6.20 (homophones sentences list), spelling journals
Teaching activity	Dictate sentences from the homophones sentences list. Choose homophones that are being spelt incorrectly in writing. Check them together and add tricky ones to pupils' personal spelling lists.

Lesson	Year 6, block 4, lesson 8
Lesson type	Revise
Lesson focus	**Proofreading**
Resources needed	Examples of pupils' own work
Teaching activity	Go over some of the tips for proofreading and ask pupils to apply them to passages of their own work.

Block 4 – spring second half term

Lesson	Year 6, block 4, lesson 9
Lesson type	Learn
Lesson focus	**Strategies for learning words: words from personal and statutory lists**
Resources needed	Spelling journals
Teaching activity	Using the range of strategies already taught, pupils continue to learn groups of words using effective strategies: • Pyramid words • Trace, copy and replicate • Look, say, cover, write, check • Drawing around the word to show the shape • Drawing an image around the word • Words without vowels • Any other methods that work

Lesson	Year 6, block 4, lesson 10
Lesson type	Assess
Lesson focus	**Words from statutory and personal lists**
Resources needed	Statutory word lists for Years 5 and 6 (page 48), personal spelling lists, spelling journals
Teaching activity	Test pupils' knowledge of statutory words as a class. Pupils mark their words, identifying errors and selecting words for further learning. Pupils work with a partner to test personal spellings and identify words that still need to be learnt.

Lesson	Year 6, block 4, lesson 11
Lesson type	Revise
Lesson focus	**Generating words from prefixes and roots**
Resources needed	Dictionaries, spelling journals
Teaching activity	Revise the terms 'etymology', 'prefix' and 'root'. Use the word *arachnophobia* to discuss how the etymology helps us to understand the meaning. If necessary, look up the prefix 'arachno' and the root 'phobia' to model the process. Pupils work in groups and use a dictionary to generate other words with the same prefix or the same root. They record these words in their spelling journals. At the end of the session share some of the words and their definitions.

Block 4 – spring second half term

Lesson	Year 6, block 4, lesson 12
Lesson type	Practise/Apply
Lesson focus	**Generating words from prefixes and roots**
Resources needed	Supporting Resource 6.21 (list of words with prefixes), spelling journals or paper for posters
Teaching activity	In pairs, pupils take one of the words from the list provided and repeat the activity modelled in the last lesson. They record the words in their spelling journals or as a poster.

Lesson	Year 6, block 4, lesson 13
Lesson type	Learn
Lesson focus	**Strategies for learning words: words from personal and statutory word lists**
Resources needed	Statutory word list for Years 5 and 6 (page 48), personal spelling lists for each pupil, spelling journals
Teaching activity	The emphasis in this lesson is on securing as many of the statutory words as possible. However, some pupils may also need to focus on their personal lists, either because they are already secure with the Year 5-6 list or because there are more common words that need to be secured. Use the range of learning strategies previously taught. <ul><li>Pyramid words</li><li>Trace, copy and replicate</li><li>Look, say, cover, write, check</li><li>Drawing around the word to show the shape</li><li>Drawing an image around the word</li><li>Words without vowels</li><li>Any other methods that work</li></ul>

Lesson	Year 6, block 4, lesson 14
Lesson type	Assess
Lesson focus	**Words from statutory word lists**
Resources needed	Statutory word list for Years 5 and 6 (page 48), personal spelling lists for each pupil, spelling journals
Teaching activity	Pupils work with a spelling partner to test each other on the statutory words that they have learnt over this half term. They update records of spellings learnt in their spelling journals.

Year 6 Term 3 overview

Block 5 – summer first half term

Week 1	Lesson 1 Teach **Strategies for learning words: rare GPCs from statutory word list**	Lesson 2 Practise **Strategies for learning words: rare GPCs from statutory word list**	Lesson 3 Apply/Assess **Rare GPCs from statutory word list**
Week 2	Lesson 4 Revise **Strategies at the point of writing: Have a go**	Lesson 5 Practise/Apply **Strategies at the point of writing: Have a go**	
Week 3	Lesson 6 Learn **Strategies for learning words: words from statutory and personal spelling lists**	Lesson 7 Assess **Words from statutory and personal spelling lists**	
Week 4	Lesson 8 Teach **Words ending in 'ant', '-ance and '-ancy'**	Lesson 9 Practise **Words ending in 'ant', '-ance and '-ancy'**	
Week 5	Lesson 10 Practise **Words ending in 'ant', '-ance and '-ancy'**	Lesson 11 Teach **Proofreading own writing independently**	Lesson 12 Practise/Apply **Proofreading own writing independently**
Week 6	Lesson 13 Revise **Root words and meaning**	Lesson 14 Practise **Root words and meaning**	

Block 6 – summer second half term

Week 1	Lesson 1 Revise **Spellings taught last half term**	Lesson 2 Revise **Spellings taught last half term**	Lesson 3 Assess **Spellings taught last half term**
Week 2	Lesson 4 Learn **Strategies for learning words: words from statutory and personal spelling lists**	Lesson 5 Learn **Strategies for learning words: words from statutory and personal spelling lists**	Lesson 6 Assess **Words from statutory and personal spelling lists: pair testing**
Week 3	Lesson 7 Teach **Words ending '-ent', '-ence' and '-ency'**	Lesson 8 Practise **Words ending '-ent', '-ence' and '-ency'**	Lesson 9 Practise **Words ending '-ent', '-ence' and '-ency'**
Week 4	Lesson 10 Assess **Words ending '-ent', '-ence' and '-ency'**	Lesson 11 Learn **Strategies for learning words: words from statutory and personal spelling lists**	Lesson 12 Learn **Strategies for learning words: words from statutory and personal spelling lists**
Week 5	Lesson 13 Assess **Words from statutory and personal spelling lists**	Lesson 14 Teach **Homophones (*draught/ draft, dissent/descent, precede/proceed, wary/ weary*)**	Lesson 15 Practise **Homophones (*draught/ draft, dissent/descent, precede/proceed, wary/ weary*)**
Week 6	Lesson 16 Apply **Homophones (*draught/ draft, dissent/descent, precede/proceed, wary/ weary*): dictation**	Lesson 17 Learn **Strategies for learning words: commonly misspelt homophones**	Lesson 18 Apply **Strategies for learning words: commonly misspelt homophones**

Block 5 – summer first half term

Lesson	Year 6, block 5, lesson 1
Lesson type	Teach
Lesson focus	**Strategies for learning words: rare grapheme-phoneme correspondences (GPCs) from statutory word list**
Resources needed	Supporting Resource 6.22 (*telephone* word web), statutory word list for Years 5 and 6 (page 48), spelling journals
Teaching activity	The first part of this term is designed to allow teachers to plan for structured revision and learning of the statutory words and other key words, prior to the spelling SATs. In this session, focus on words from the statutory spelling list for Year 5-6 which are very tricky for pupils. This might be particular words which they keep forgetting, or a pattern in words, such as unstressed vowels or a particular letter string. Model taking one of these words and exploring how they are built up in a variety of ways. These could include the following: • Breaking the word into syllables and then segmenting the phonemes within a syllable. • Breaking the word into morphemes (prefix/root/suffix). • Identifying words within words. • Making links between the word and other words that they know, for example: other words with the same prefix/suffix; words that sound the same (analogy); words with the same or a similar root. • Identifying parts of the word that are really tricky to spell. • Thinking of ideas for remembering that part. • Finding the meaning and derivation of the word. • Writing a short sentence or phrase to help remember it (mnemonic).

Lesson	Year 6, block 5, lesson 2
Lesson type	Practise
Lesson focus	**Strategies for learning words: rare GPCs from statutory word list**
Resources needed	Statutory word list for Years 5 and 6 (page 48), spelling journals
Teaching activity	Pupils identify their own tricky words from the statutory word list. They make a word web like the example in the previous lesson in their spelling journals, to help them to remember and understand the word.

Lesson	Year 6, block 5, lesson 3
Lesson type	Assess
Lesson focus	**Rare GPCs from statutory word lists**
Resources needed	Statutory word lists (see page 48), spelling journals
Teaching activity	Test the whole class on the tricky words they have been learning. Once checked, ask pupils to show and talk about their word webs to find any common errors.

Block 5 – summer first half term

Lesson	Year 6, block 5, lesson 4
Lesson type	Revise
Lesson focus	**Strategies at the point of writing: Have a go**
Resources needed	Supporting Resource 6.2 (Have a go sheet)
Teaching activity	Pupils will be very familiar with using Have a go sheets in whatever form you have established in your class. The purpose of this session is to challenge pupils to link what they have been learning about the morphology and etymology of words to their attempts at words they want to spell. Take some examples of more challenging words that have been spelt incorrectly from pupils' writing. Model trying to spell them in three or four different ways and, each time, be very explicit about the strategy that you are applying and your thinking about the morphology and etymology of the word. You might model<ul><li>identifying a prefix, root or suffix that you know and trying that spelling.</li><li>linking the word to other known words in terms of meaning or word strings.</li><li>applying some of the conventions pupils know, for example: changing a 'y' to an 'i' or when to use 'ie'/'ei'</li><li>identifying parts of the word that don't look right and focusing on them.</li></ul>

Lesson	Year 6, block 5, lesson 5
Lesson type	Practise/Apply
Lesson focus	**Strategies at the point of writing: Have a go**
Resources needed	Supporting Resource 6.2 (Have a go sheet)
Teaching activity	Pupils identify words from their own writing that they need to correct. Make sure they are more challenging, polysyllabic words. Using some of the strategies that were modelled in the previous session, pupils have a go with three or four attempts. At the end of the session, ask pupils to talk through their attempts, showing which strategies they have applied.

Lesson	Year 6, block 5, lesson 6
Lesson type	Learn
Lesson focus	**Strategies for learning words: words from statutory and personal spelling lists**
Resources needed	Statutory word list for Years 5 and 6 (see page 48), personal spelling lists, spelling journals
Teaching activity	Pupils learn spellings from their personal and statutory word lists. You may need to direct pupils depending on how many of the statutory words they know. These are the last learning sessions before the spelling SAT, so ensure that pupils are focused on the most important words for them. Remind pupils of the strategies they can use to learn their words.

Block 5 – summer first half term

Lesson	Year 6, block 5, lesson 7
Lesson type	Assess
Lesson focus	**Words from statutory and personal spelling lists**
Resources needed	Statutory word list for Years 5 and 6 (page 48), personal spelling lists, spelling journals
Teaching activity	Pupils work with partners to test spellings and identify words that still need to be learnt. You may need to provide an extra session for pupils to learn these words.

Lesson	Year 6, block 5, lesson 8
Lesson type	Teach
Lesson focus	**Words ending '-ant', '-ance' and '-ancy'**
Resources needed	Supporting Resource 6.23 (example table) and 6.24 (cards with '-ance' words)
Teaching activity	Explain that pupils are going to explore another tricky word ending. This one is tricky because they have to choose if it's '-ance' or '-ence'. This half term pupils will focus on the '-ance', '-ant' and '-ancy' words and next half term they will look at those with '-ent', '-ence' and '-ency'. Model how pupils can create a table which shows the application of the conventions about adding '-ance'/'-ancy'. Use sets of cards with the '-ance' words. Show pupils how to take a word and decide which column to put it in based on the reason it takes '-ance'. Do a few examples together. **Notes:** • '-ance'/'-ancy' are used where the root word ends in '-ant' (*observant/observance, expectant/expectance*). • If the root word can add the ending '-ation', then these words will usually take '-ance'/'-ancy'. • If the related verb ends in '-y', '-ure,' '-ear' or '-ate', then the noun will take '-ance'. • If the stem of the word ends in a hard /c/ or /g/ sound, then it takes '-ance'.

Lesson	Year 6, block 5, lesson 9
Lesson type	Practise
Lesson focus	**Words ending '-ant', '-ance' and '-ancy'**
Resources needed	Supporting Resource 6.24 (cards with '-ance' words)
Teaching activity	Pupils work in pairs to continue the activity modelled in the previous lesson using words from the cards.

Block 5 – summer first half term

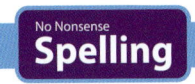

Lesson	Year 6, block 5, lesson 10
Lesson type	Practise
Lesson focus	**Words ending '-ant', '-ance' and '-ancy'**
Resources needed	Supporting Resource 6.24 (cards with '-ance' words)
Teaching activity	Pupils work in pairs to continue the activity from the previous lesson. They try to do as many words as possible from the cards provided. At the end of this session share what pupils have discovered during the two lessons and try to draw any generalisations about spelling choice.

Lesson	Year 6, block 5, lesson 11
Lesson type	Teach
Lesson focus	**Proofreading own writing independently**
Resources needed	Examples of pupils' own writing
Teaching activity	Revisit strategies that pupils already know for proofreading their writing. The focus for this session is on demonstrating that pupils can proofread independently. Explain that at the end of the next spelling session, pupils will need to explain how they have used proofreading skills to improve the spelling of their writing. Give pupils the rest of this session and the following lesson to proofread their own writing, identify incorrect spellings and correct them.

Lesson	Year 6, block 5, lesson 12
Lesson type	Practise/Apply
Lesson focus	**Proofreading own writing independently**
Resources needed	Examples of pupils' own writing
Teaching activity	Pupils continue to proofread their writing. At the end of this session pupils explain to their spelling partners how they have used proofreading to improve their writing.

Block 5 – summer first half term

Lesson	Year 6, block 5, lesson 13
Lesson type	Revise
Lesson focus	**Root words and meaning**
Resources needed	Supporting Resource 6.26 (root word list)
Teaching activity	Remind pupils about the meaning of the term 'etymology'. This lesson focuses on the etymology of root words and how it helps us to both spell and understand meaning. Give pairs of pupils a root word from list provided. They need to do the following: 1 Find the meaning of the root and where it came from (using a dictionary or the internet) 2 Build as many words as they can by adding prefixes and suffixes to the root. In each case, make sure they can define the word.

Lesson	Year 6, block 5, lesson 14
Lesson type	Practise/Apply
Lesson focus	**Root words and meaning**
Resources needed	Supporting Resource 6.25 (roots, prefix and suffix quiz)
Teaching activity	Take the quiz as a class, discussing the answers to draw learning together. Suggest that pupils make their own multiple-choice quiz using the words they have derived.

Block 6 – summer second half term

Lesson	Year 6, block 6, lessons 1 and 2
Lesson type	Revise
Lesson focus	**Spellings taught last half term**
Resources needed	Statutory word list for Years 5 and 6 (page 48)
Teaching activity	Identify elements from the previous half term that need consolidation. Revise key activities needing consolidation identified in previous session.

Lesson	Year 6, block 6, lesson 3
Lesson type	Assess
Lesson focus	**Spellings taught last half term**
Resources needed	Statutory word list for Years 5 and 6 (see page 48), personal spelling lists, spelling journals
Teaching activity	Pupils work with a partner to test spellings and identify words that still need to be learnt. Set up words from statutory lists to be learnt by each pupil across this half term.

Lesson	Year 6, block 6, lesson 4
Lesson type	Learn
Lesson focus	**Strategies for learning words: words from statutory and personal spelling lists**
Resources needed	Statutory word list for Years 5 and 6 (see page 48), personal spelling lists, spelling journals
Teaching activity	Pupils learn spellings from their personal and statutory word lists. This session and the one which follows provides an opportunity to focus on any key words that pupils struggled with in the SATs test, as well as on their personal word lists.

Lesson	Year 6, block 6, lesson 5
Lesson type	Learn
Lesson focus	**Strategies for learning words: words from statutory and personal spelling lists**
Resources needed	Statutory word list for Years 5 and 6 (page 48), personal spelling lists, spelling journals
Teaching activity	Pupils continue the work from the last lesson to learn spellings from their personal and statutory word lists.

No Nonsense Spelling

Block 6 – summer second half term

Lesson	Year 6, block 6, lesson 6
Lesson type	Assess
Lesson focus	**Words from statutory and personal spelling lists: pair testing**
Resources needed	Statutory word list for Years 5 and 6 (see page 48), personal spelling lists, spelling journals
Teaching activity	Pupils work with a partner to test spellings and identify words which still need to be learnt. You may need to provide an extra session for pupils to learn these words.

Lesson	Year 6, block 6, lesson 7
Lesson type	Teach
Lesson focus	**Words ending '-ent', '-ence' and '-ency'**
Resources needed	Supporting Resources 6.27 (example table) and 6.28 ('-ence' word cards)
Teaching activity	Explain that pupils are going to explore another tricky word ending. This one is tricky because they have to choose if its '-ance' or '-ence'. Last half term they focused on the '-ance', '-ant' and '-ancy' words; this half term they will look at those with '-ent', '-ence' and '-ency'. See what pupils can rememer about the use of '-ance' (see Year 6, block 5, lessons 8, 9, 10). Tell pupils they are going to repeat the activity but with different headings. Model how they can create a table (see example provided) showing the application of the conventions about adding '-ence' and '-ency'. Use sets of the '-ence' words cards. Show pupils how to take a word and decide which column to put it in based on the reason it takes '–ence'. Do a few examples together. **Notes:** • If the root verb ends in '-ere', for example *interfere*, then it takes '-ence'. • If the root verb has a stressed '-er' ending, then it takes '-ence', for example, *infer*. • If the word contains the syllables 'cid', 'fid', 'sid' or 'vid' immediately before the ending, the correct suffix is '-ence', for example, *confidence*. • If the stem of the word ends in a soft 'c' (pronounced like 'c' in *cell*) or a soft 'g' (pronounced like 'g' in *gel*), then the ending will be '-ence', for example, *innocence*.

Block 6 – summer second half term

Lesson	Year 6, block 6, lesson 8
Lesson type	Practise
Lesson focus	**Words ending '-ent', '-ence' and '-ency'**
Resources needed	Supporting Resources 6.27 (example table) and 6.28 ('-ence' word cards)
Teaching activity	Children work in pairs to continue the activity modelled in the previous lesson using the word cards provided.

Lesson	Year 6, block 6, lesson 9
Lesson type	Practise
Lesson focus	**Words ending '-ent', '-ence' and '-ency'**
Resources needed	Supporting Resources 6.27 (example table) and 6.28 ('-ence' word cards)
Teaching activity	Pupils work in pairs and continue the activity from the previous lesson. They try to do as many words as possible from the list. At the end of this session share what pupils have discovered during the two lessons and try to draw any generalisations about spelling choice.

Lesson	Year 6, block 6, lesson 10
Lesson type	Assess
Lesson focus	**Words ending '-ent', '-ence' and '-ency'**
Resources needed	Supporting Resources 6.24 ('-ance' word cards) and 6.28 ('-ence' word cards)
Teaching activity	Do a spelling test, using a range of the words from the last two sessions and those on '-ance' from last half term (pages 39–40). See how many the pupils can spell correctly. You may need to display the conventions to support them. Concentrate on some of the more common words that they are likely to use more often.

Lesson	Year 6, block 6, lessons 11 and 12
Lesson type	Learn
Lesson focus	**Stategies for learning words: selected words from statutory and personal spelling lists**
Resources needed	Statutory word list for Years 5 and 6 (see page 48), personal spelling lists, spelling journals
Teaching activity	Pupils learn spellings from their personal and statutory word lists over two sessions. This session, and the one which follows it, provides an opportunity to focus on any key words that pupils struggled with in the SATs test and also to focus on personal word lists.

Block 6 – summer second half term

Lesson	Year 6, block 6, lesson 13
Lesson type	Assess
Lesson focus	**Words from statutory and personal spelling lists**
Resources needed	Statutory word list for Years 5 and 6 (page 48), personal spelling lists for each pupil, spelling journals
Teaching activity	Pupils work with partners to test spellings and identify words that still need to be learnt. They update the records of spellings learnt in their spelling journals.

Lesson	Year 6, block 6, lesson 14
Lesson type	Teach
Lesson focus	**Homophones (*draught/draft, dissent/descent, precede/proceed, wary/weary*)**
Resources needed	Supporting Resource 6.29 (homophones list), spelling journals
Teaching activity	Introduce the new homophones on the list provided. Pupils work in pairs to discuss and research the two different meanings of these words. They try with their partner to think of some clever ways of remembering which word is which. Share ideas and pupils record them in their spelling journals.

Lesson	Year 6, block 6, lesson 15
Lesson type	Practise
Lesson focus	**Homophones (*draught/draft, dissent/descent, precede/proceed, wary/weary*)**
Resources needed	Supporting Resource 6.29 (homophones list), spelling journals
Teaching activity	Pupils put the new homophones into sentences, using them correctly.

Lesson	Year 6, block 6, lesson 16
Lesson type	Assess
Lesson focus	**Homophones (*draught/draft, dissent/descent, precede/proceed, wary/weary*): dictation**
Resources needed	Supporting Resource 6.20 (homophones sentences list)
Teaching activity	Dictate sentences from the homophones sentences list. Use these sentences and pupils' own writing to identify a group of tricky homophones that each pupil needs to learn.

Block 6 – summer second half term

Lesson	Year 6, block 6, lesson 17
Lesson type	Learn
Lesson focus	**Strategies for learning words: commonly misspelt homophones**
Resources needed	Spelling journals
Teaching activity	Pupils apply the range of strategies they know for learning the tricky homophones identified in the previous lesson and try to secure their spellings.

Lesson	Year 6, block 6, lesson 18
Lesson type	Apply
Lesson focus	**Strategies for learning words: commonly misspelt homophones**
Resources needed	Spelling journals
Teaching activity	Look at all the homophones being learnt in the class. In pairs, pupils make up their own sentences for the tricky homophones and use these as dictations for another pair. You could swap the homophone words around between the pairs so that they are assessing each other, rather than using the ones they learnt to write the sentences.

Statutory word list for Years 5 and 6

accommodate
accompany
according
achieve
aggressive
amateur
ancient
apparent
appreciate
attached
available
average
awkward
bargain
bruise
category
cemetery
committee
communicate
community
competition
conscience
conscious
controversy
convenience
correspond
criticise (critic + ise)
curiosity
definite
desperate
determined
develop
dictionary
disastrous
embarrass
environment

equip (-ped, -ment)
especially
exaggerate
excellent
existence
explanation
familiar
foreign
forty
frequently
government
guarantee
harass
hindrance
identity
immediately
interfere
interrupt
language
leisure
lightning (h)
marvellous
mischievous
muscle (h)
necessary
neighbour
nuisance
occupy
occur
opportunity
parliament
persuade
physical
prejudice
privilege
profession

programme
pronunciation
queue
recognise
recommend
restaurant
rhyme
rhythm
sacrifice
secretary
shoulder
signature
sincere(ly)
soldier
stomach
sufficient
suggest
symbol (h)
system
temperature
thorough
twelfth
variety
vegetable
vehicle
yacht

Year 6 Supporting Resources

Error Analysis template 6.1

Name _____   Class _____   Date _____

Common exception words	GPC (includes rare GPCs and vowel digraphs)	Homophones	Prefixes and suffixes	Word endings	Other

Have a go template 6.2

My column	Teacher's column	My column	Teacher's column

GPC chart 6.3

These charts show the phonemes of English represented by the International Phonetic Alphabet together with their common grapheme representations. All Phase 5 GPCs are included together with other less common grapheme choices needed in Year 2 and above. The correspondences in the table are based on Received Pronunciation and could be significantly different in other accents. One example word is provided for each phoneme to support teachers unfamiliar with IPA. Other examples can be found in Appendix 1 of the National Curriculum.

Consonant GPCs

/b/ bat	/d/ dog	/ð/ mother	/dʒ/ jug	/f/ fish	/g/ goat	/h/ hand	/j/ yawn	/k/ cat	/l/ and /əl/ lamp, bottle	/m/ mouse	/n/ nail
b bb	d dd	th	j g ge dge	f ff ph	g gg gu gue	h	y	c k ck ch q que	l ll le el al il	m mm mb	n nn kn gn pn mn

/ŋ/ wing	/θ/ thumb	/p/ pin	/r/ rain	/s/ sun	/ʃ/ ship	/t/ tap	/tʃ/ chick	/v/ van	/w/ watch	/z/ zip
ng n(k)	th	p	r rr wr	s ss se sc c ce	sh ch ti ci ss(ion, ure) s (ion, ure)	t tt	ch tch t	v ve	w wh u	z zz ze s se x

Note: The letter **x** in English frequently represents 2 adjacent consonant phonemes /k/ and /s/, for example in the word **box**.

Vowel GPCs

/aː/ arm	/ɒ/ hot	/æ/ cat	/aɪ/ pie	/aʊ/ cow	/ɛ/ hen	/eɪ/ day	/ɛə/ pair	/əʊ/ boat	/ɪ/ pin
ar a	o a	a	igh i-e ie i y	ow ou	e ea	ai ay a-e a aigh ei eigh ey	air are ear	ow oa oe o-e o	i y e

/ɪə/ cheer	/iː/ bean	/ɔː/ fork	/ɔɪ/ boy	/ʊ/ book	/ʊə/ cure	/uː/ blue	/ʌ/ cup	/ɜː/ girl
ear eer ere	ea ee e-e ie y ey e ei eo	or oor ore aw au our a al ar	oy oi	oo u oul	ure our	oo u-e ue ew ui ou ough	u o	er ir ur or ear

Note: The symbol /ə/, known as "schwa" represents the unstressed phoneme in many English words. It can be spelt in many different ways, for example **er** as in farm**er**.

Year 6 – Block 1 – Lesson 5 6.4

-able	-ible
-ably	-ibly

Year 6 – Block 1 – Lessons 5 and 6 6.5

horrible	adorable	Additional words
terrible	forgivable	incredibly
possible	disposable	sensibly
edible	enjoyable	reliably
reversible	valuable	respectably
invincible	breakable	agreeably
legible	identifiable	enviably

Year 6 – Block 1 – Lessons 8 and 9 6.6

-ed	-ing
-ence	-al

refer
prefer
transfer

Year 6 – Block 3 – Lesson 10 6.15

Instructions for proofreading someone else's writing:

1. Swap writing books with your spelling partner.
2. Proofread the last two pieces of work.
3. Underline with a wiggly line any words which you think may be spelt incorrectly.
4. Feed back to your partner.
5. Work together to correct spellings.
6. Add words to learn to personal list in spelling journal.

Year 6 – Block 3 – Lesson 13 6.16

bi	aqua	super	auto
trans	tele	circum	extra
pro	anti	semi	aero

Year 6 – Block 3 – Lesson 13 6.17

Prefix	Meaning/derivation	Word 1	Word 2	Word 3
bi-	two (Latin)	bicycle	biped	binary

Year 6 – Block 4 – Lesson 5 6.18

dessert	desert
stationery	stationary
complement	compliment
principle	principal
prophet	profit

Year 6 – Block 3 – Lessons 7–9 6.13

Word	Root word	Meaning	Why '-cial' or '-tial'?

Year 6 – Block 3 – Lessons 7–9 6.14

'-cial' words		
official	commercial	glacial
special	facial	social
artificial	financial	racial
'-tial' words		
partial	confidential	essential
influential	substantial	torrential
preferential	residential	quintessential

Year 6 – Block 2 – Lessons 9–11 6.10

vicious	precious	conscious
delicious	malicious	suspicious
ambitious	cautious	fictitious
infectious	nutritious	

Year 6 – Block 3 – Lesson 1 6.11

I take it you already know
Of tough and bough and cough and dough?
Others may stumble, but not you,
On hiccough, thorough, lough and through?

Year 6 – Block 3 – Lessons 2 and 3 6.12

bough	cough	dough
enough	bought	plough
though	drought	sought
thought	tough	thorough
rough	although	brought
ought		

Year 6 – Block 1 – Lessons 14 and 15   6.7

Proofreading checklist

Does my writing make sense? ☐
Are there any really obvious spelling errors? ☐
Check each sentence carefully. ☐
Underline any possible errors. ☐
Have a go at correcting the errors you have identified. ☐

Year 6 – Block 2 – Lesson 4   6.8

The advice is to stay indoors.	Police advise all residents to stay indoors.
Please turn off that device.	Can you devise a plan to escape?
Spelling practice is extremely important.	I practise my handwriting every day.
It costs £60 for a TV licence.	James Bond … licensed to kill.

Year 6 – Block 2 – Lesson 5   6.9

advice	advise
device	devise
practice	practise
licence	license

Year 6 – Block 4 – Lesson 6 6.19

All homophones for KS2

brake/break
grate/great
eight/ate
weight/wait
son/sun
here/hear
knot/not
meat/meet
missed/mist
heard/herd
through/threw
peace/piece
main/mane
fair/fare
scene/seen
male/mail
bawl/ball
whether/weather
affect/effect
medal/meddle
isle/aisle
aloud/allowed
affect/effect

past/passed.
altar/alter
ascent/assent
bridle/bridal
led/lead
steal/steel
cereal/serial
father/farther
guessed/guest
morning/mourning
who's/whose
advice/advise
device/devise
licence/license
practice/practise
compliment/complement
desert/dessert
principal/principle
profit/prophet
stationery/stationary
draft/draught
dissent/descent
precede/proceed

No Nonsense Spelling

Year 6 – Block 4 – Lesson 7 and Block 6 – Lesson 16   6.20

1. I'll be walking down the aisle on my wedding day.
2. The runner was so hungry, he ate eight sandwiches.
3. The cyclist didn't use his brake in time, causing his bicycle to break when it hit the wall.
4. The web developer designed a site that could test your sight to see if you were colourblind.
5. The knot was not tied well, so it came undone.
6. The person who delivered the mail was a young male.
7. The butcher went to meet the farmer from whom he buys his meat.
8. The driver missed the road he was supposed to turn down as the mist meant he couldn't see the road sign.
9. The family was still in mourning the morning after the funeral.
10. The truck driver passed a couple of cyclists before driving past a parked car.
11. The beauty queen said her favourite food was a piece of pie and that she'd like to see world peace.
12. The film's final scene was something that had to be seen to be believed.
13. The car full of stationery was stationary.
14. Who's that person over there? Is he the man whose wallet was stolen?
15. That's a great grate you have bought.
16. I can't wait to put down this heavy weight.
17. My son loves to watch the sun set.
18. Have you heard that herd of cows?
19. Tom threw the ball and it went straight through the window.
20. The horse fair was held in the main street. Manes were flying as the race started.
21. The fares charged at the fair were really unfair!
22. The baby started to bawl when his brother took away his bouncy ball.
23. It doesn't matter whether the weather is warm or not. I have my coat.
24. The effect of your bad mood is that I get grumpy. That affects everyone!
25. Grandad always told me not to meddle with his medals.
26. We are not allowed to shout our ideas aloud in class.
27. The altar in church hasn't altered for 100 years.
28. When I assented to climbing Mount Everest, I had no idea how steep the ascent would be.
29. The horse needed a white bridle for the bridal carriage.
30. The police led me to see the lead missing from the church roof.
31. Steel is a metal that is not worth stealing.
32. I always settle down to watch my favourite TV serial with a bowl of my favourite cereal.
33. My father and I drifted farther apart over the years.
34. Who would have guessed that the special guest would be you!
35. The advice to all parents is to advise their children not to go with strangers.
36. I wish someone could devise a device that could let us travel in time.
37. In order to license the ownership of gerbils, everyone will have to apply for a licence.
38. The Doctors' practice will be closed, to allow for the staff to practise their handwriting.
39. May I compliment you on the complementary colours you are wearing today?
40. There are not many options for dessert in the desert.
41. In principle, we have no problems with appointing a child as principal of the school.
42. We will need a prophet to find a way of making this business make a profit again!
43. The descent from the mountain was easy as there was no more dissent.
44. In order to proceed, you need to read the notes and the preceding guidance.

Year 6 – Block 4 – Lesson 12 — 6.21

autobiography
binoculars
archaeology
telecommunication
hydroelectric
microscope

Year 6 – Block 5 – Lesson 1 — 6.22

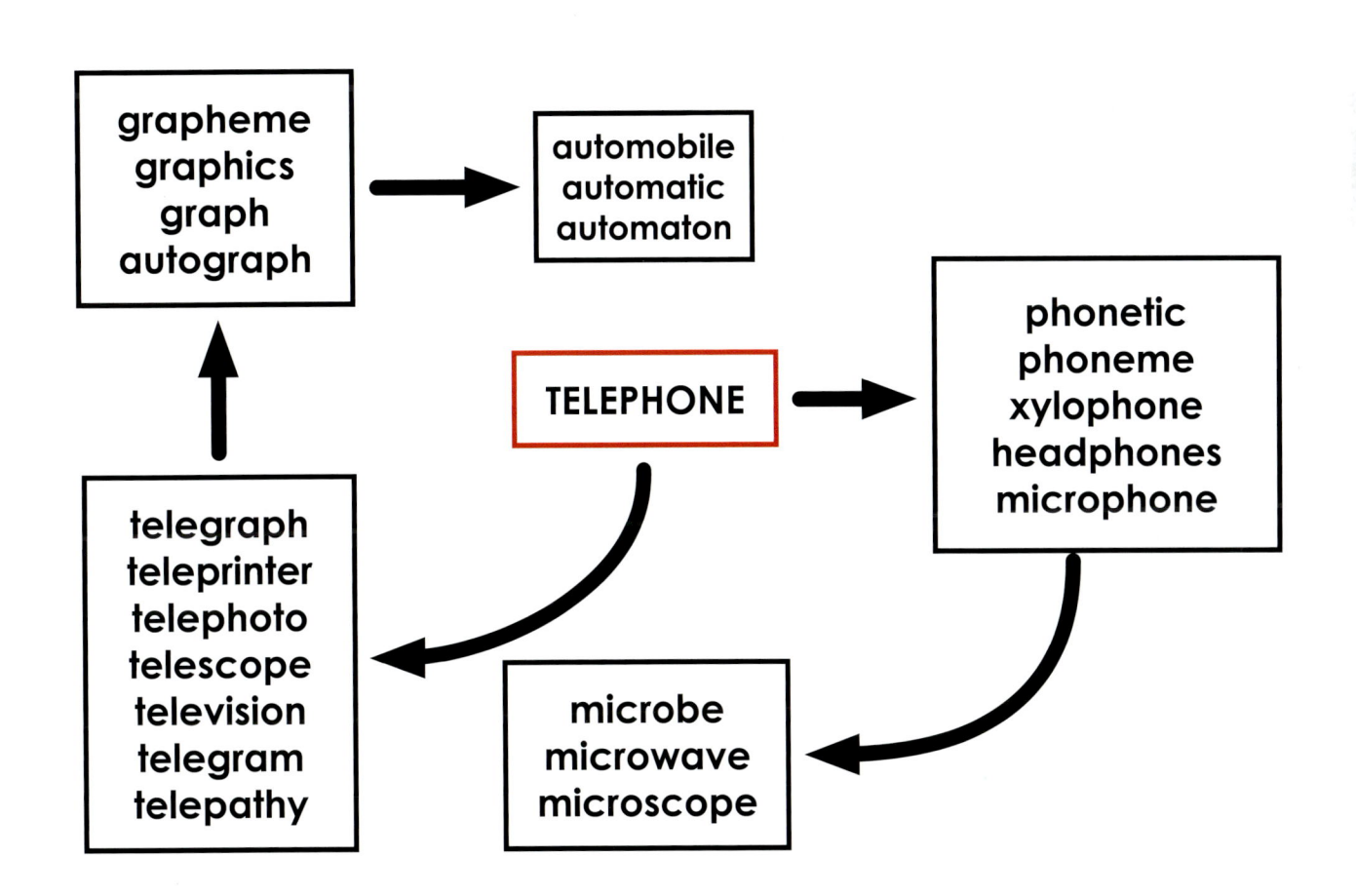

grapheme
graphics
graph
autograph

→

automobile
automatic
automaton

TELEPHONE →

phonetic
phoneme
xylophone
headphones
microphone

telegraph
teleprinter
telephoto
telescope
television
telegram
telepathy

microbe
microwave
microscope

Year 6 – Block 5 – Lesson 8   6.23

Root word ends in '-ant'	Root verb ends in '-y'	Root verb ends in '-ure'	Root verb ends in '-ear'	Root verb ends in '-ate'	Stem of '-ance' word ends in hard 'c' (cat)	Stem of '-ance' word ends in hard 'g' (goat)	Exceptions

Year 6 – Block 5 – Lessons 8-10 and Block 6 – Lesson 10   6.24

acquaintance	appliance	inheritance
abundance	deviate	deviance
acceptance	dominate	dominance
allowance	hesitate	hesitance
assistance	tolerate	tolerance
attendance	significance	endurance
balance	elegance	insurance
circumstance	abundance	resistance
countenance	performance	appearance
distance	guidance	clearance
perseverance	allowance	forbearance
assistance	circumstance	instance

No Nonsense Spelling

No Nonsense Spelling Programme

Year 6 – Block 5 – Lesson 13   6.25

1. If the prefix **inter-** means **between**, the portion of time between acts of play or during a concert is called an...
   - a bicycle
   - b intermission
   - c international
   - d audience

2. If the prefix **crede-** means to **believe**, if you can believe someone, then that person has good...
   - a credibility
   - b counterfeit
   - c cycle
   - d credit

3. If the prefix **dict-** means **speak**, a person's manner of speaking is called...
   - a benefit
   - b diction
   - c dictionary
   - d prescription

4. If the prefix **tract-** means **to drag, draw**, the act of drawing or pulling a thing is known as...
   - a traction
   - b attractive
   - c demagogue
   - d incredulous

5. If the prefix **inter-** means **between**, the trade between nations is referred to as...
   - a international
   - b telescope
   - c encyclopedia
   - d television

6. If the root **script** means to **write**, a doctor's hand-written instruction for the preparation of medicine is known as a...
   - a manuscript
   - b demagogue
   - c prescription
   - d television

7. If the suffix **-script** means **to write**, handwritten or typed text is also known as a...
   - a prescription
   - b predict
   - c manuscript
   - d attractive

8. If the suffix **-cede** means **to go, to yield**, to receive more in return than you thought you would, then your expectations are...
   - a exceeded
   - b proceed
   - c succeed
   - d preceded

9 If the suffix **-dict** means **speak**, when a person on a jury speaks and gives a truthful decision or judgment, the person is stating the...
 a   dictionary
 b   predict
 c   verdict
 d   diction

10 If the prefix **tele-** means **distance, from afar**, communication over a distance by cable, telegraph or telephone lines is known as...
 a   contrary
 b   telecommunication
 c   auditorium
 d   incredulous

11 If the prefix **audi-** means **to hear**, if you hear something clearly it is...
 a   external
 b   audible
 c   anachronism
 d   democracy

12 If the root **demo** means **people**, a widespread occurrence of a disease within a group of people is called an...
 a   scribble
 b   external
 c   verdict
 d   epidemic

13 If the prefix **vita-** means **life**, a compilation of several organic compounds essential for living organisms are known as...
 a   flexible
 b   autograph
 c   benefit
 d   vitamins

Year 6 – Block 5 – Lesson 14 6.26

| cyclo | chrono | tract | dict |
| script | fac | port | struct |

Year 6 – Block 6 – Lessons 7–9 6.27

Root verb ends in '-ere'	Root verb ends in stressed '-er' syllable	Word contains 'cid', 'fid', 'sid', 'vid'	Stem of '-ence' word ends in soft /c/ (*cell*) or soft /g/ (*gel*)	Exceptions

63

Year 6 – Block 6 – Lessons 7–10 6.28

adherence	preference	adolescence
coherence	transference	indulgence
inference	confidence	innocence
reference	evidence	intelligence
interference	incidence	licence
conference	residence	negligence
dependence	audience	patience
circumference	excellence	sentence
sequence	silence	consequence
violence	convenience	existence

Year 6 – Block 6 – Lessons 14 and 15 6.29

draught	draft
dissent	descent
precede	proceed
wary	weary